LIGHTNING
BOLT
BOOKS™

The Erie Canal

Lisa Bullard

Lerner Publications Company
Minneapolis

For Alexis,
with love

Lerner Publications Company
A division of Lerner Publishing Group, Inc.
241 First Avenue North
Minneapolis, MN 55401 U.S.A.

Website address: www.lernerbooks.com

Library of Congress Cataloging-in-Publication Data

Bullard, Lisa.
    The Erie Canal / by Lisa Bullard.
        p.   cm. — (Lightning Bolt Books™ — Famous Places)
    Includes index.
    ISBN 978–0–8225–9405–5 (lib. bdg. : alk. paper)
    1. Erie Canal (N.Y.)—Juvenile literature. 2. Erie Canal (N.Y.)—History—Juvenile literature.
    I. Title.
    HE396.E6B85 2010
    386'.4809747—dc22   2008030639

Manufactured in the United States of America
1 2 3 4 5 6 — BP — 15 14 13 12 11 10

Contents

A tugboat pushes a barge down the Erie Canal in New York.

What is the Erie Canal?

The Erie Canal is a waterway built for boats. It was one of the first canals in the United States. The canal opened an important path to the West. It linked the East Coast to the Great Lakes. People could easily travel back and forth.

The United States did not start out as a large country. In the early days, most people lived in the East.

The country needed land to grow bigger. Newcomers needed places to live. People needed space to farm.

East Coast cities such as New York were busy and crowded!

There was room to build out West. Few people lived around the Great Lakes. That land was not yet broken into states.

Large stretches of land lay beyond the East Coast. Few homes or buildings stood there.

The Appalachian Mountains blocked the way west. **People started talking about building a canal through the mountains.**

Traveling through the mountains was difficult. People thought a canal would make it easier.

One possible
canal path ran
through New York
State. It went
from the Hudson
River to Lake Erie.

This black line
traces the path
of the canal from
the Hudson River
to Lake Erie.

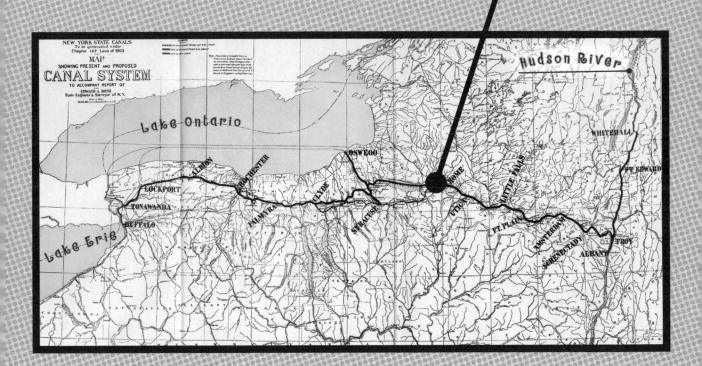

But would building this canal really help the country grow?

Difficult landscape
kept many people
from moving west.

Workers with shovels and wheelbarrows helped build the Erie Canal.

Building the Canal

DeWitt Clinton liked the canal plan. He became governor of New York in 1817. New York decided to build the Erie Canal. The builders did not have big machines back then. Men and horses would have to do the hard work. Building started on July 4, 1817. Men cut down trees to clear a path.

Workers began digging.
The canal needed to be
40 feet (12 meters) wide
and 4 feet (1.2 m) deep.

The canal was wide but not very deep. This painting shows construction workers standing in the bottom of the canal.

The canal also needed a towpath. A towpath is a trail for mules and horses. Mules and horses pulled the early canal boats. The animals walked along the trail.

The banks of the canal needed to be wide enough to give horses room to walk.

The way through the mountains was not flat. The canal path led up and down. Sometimes this change in height happened quickly.

At some places, the canal passes through steep mountains.

This boat passes through a lock on the Erie Canal.

Boats could not make these sudden big jumps. So workers had to build locks. The locks lifted the boats up and down.

In one spot, the canal path went up about 60 feet (18 m). That is about as high as a six-story building. It took five locks to raise boats that high.

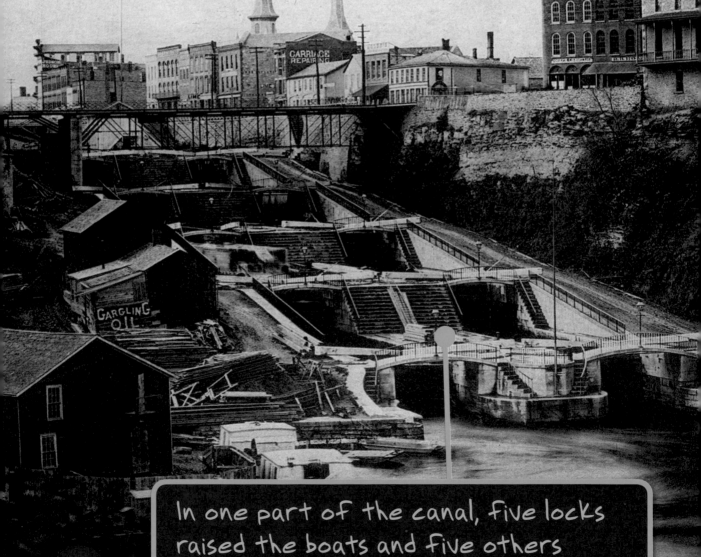

In one part of the canal, five locks raised the boats and five others lowered them—much like an escalator.

Canal water flows over an aquaduct.

The workers also built aqueducts.

An aqueduct is a bridge that carries canal waters over rivers, roads, and valleys.

A Big Success

The new canal opened on October 26, 1825. Governor Clinton led a group of canal boats from Buffalo, New York. They sailed 363 miles (584 kilometers) to Albany, New York. Then they sailed down the Hudson River to New York City. New Yorkers were very proud of their canal.

The canal was a big success.
Many people moved west on
packet boats. These boats carried
mail and passengers. The people
built cities and farms. The
country kept growing.

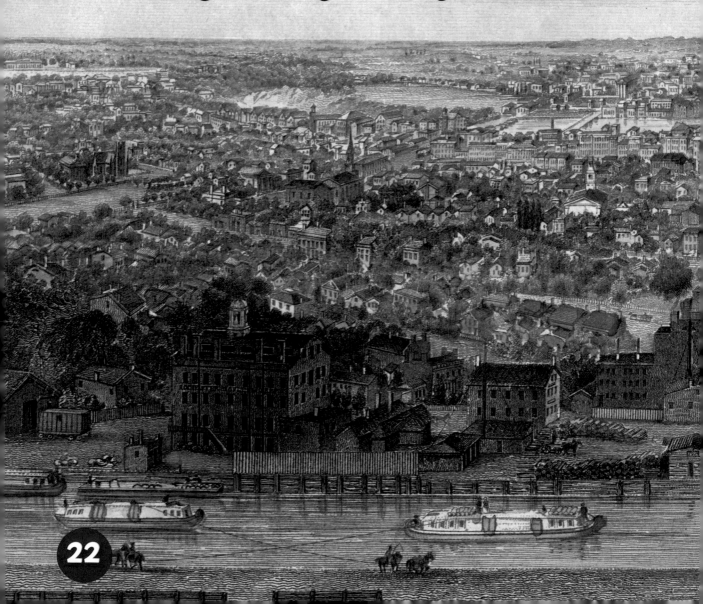

Barges carried products from west to east. The barges carried wheat, timber, and furs.

The city of Rochester, New York, grew bigger because of the canal.

Then the barges carried supplies back west to the settlers. New York City was the center of the action. It became an important city.

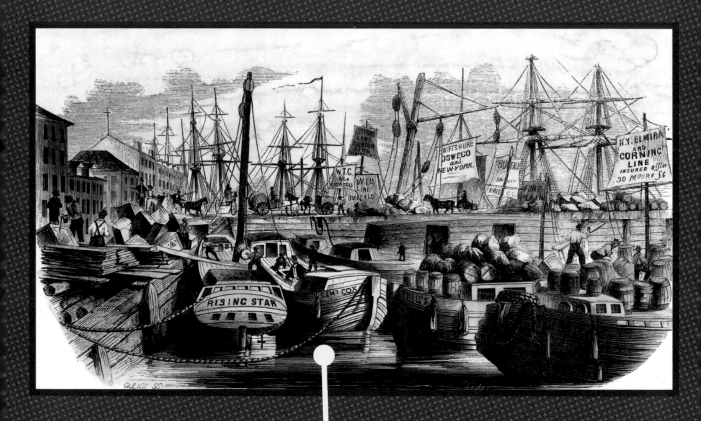

Erie Canal boats tied up on the Hudson River in New York City

Workers continued to improve the canal. They made it bigger for bigger boats. The canal stayed busy for more than one hundred years.

Canal workers had to make the Erie Canal wider to make room for bigger riverboats.

Crowds and boaters enjoy a festival on the Erie Canal.

Changes in Transportation

Railroads sprang up soon after the canal opened. Over time, trains took away more and more canal business. Other kinds of transportation such as trucks came later. Canal business finally stopped. But people have not forgotten this important part of history. **The Erie Canal is still used for boating fun.**

New York State Area

Fun Facts

- Children often led the mules or horses along the canal's towpath. These children were called hoggees.

- Part of the Erie Canal path went through a very wet area. Many mosquitoes grew there. Some of them carried a disease called malaria. Many workers became sick.

- Many people who worked on the Erie Canal were immigrants. They came to the United States from other countries. They wanted to make a new life. They were glad to get a job building the canal.

- The modern-day Erie Canal is part of a bigger waterway system. This is called the New York State Canal System.

Glossary

Appalachian Mountains: the second-largest mountain range in North America. The Appalachians spread across eastern North America from Canada to Alabama.

aqueduct: a bridge that carries canal waters over rivers, roads, and valleys

barge: a boat with a flat bottom that is used to haul freight

canal: a waterway built for boats

East Coast: the eastern part of the United States that runs along the Atlantic Ocean

governor: the person elected to run a state

Great Lakes: a chain of five lakes on the border of the United States and Canada to the west of New York and Pennsylvania

lock: a place in a canal with gates on each end, used to lift and lower boats to a different water level

packet boat: a canal boat that carried mail and passengers

towpath: a trail for mules and horses to walk on as they pulled early canal boats

transportation: something used to move people or things from one place to another

Further Reading

Armbruster, Ann. *Lake Erie*. New York: Children's Press, 1996.

Big Apple History
http://pbskids.org/bigapplehistory/building/topic1.html

EPodunk
http://www.epodunk.com/routes/erie-canal/index.html

Harness, Cheryl. *The Amazing Impossible Erie Canal*. New York: Aladdin, 1999.

Murray, Julie. *Erie Canal*. Edina, MN: Abdo, 2005.

Social Studies for Kids
http://www.socialstudiesforkids.com/articles/ushistory/eriecanal1.htm

Index

Photo Acknowledgments

The images in this book are used with the permission of: © Robert F. Sisson/National Geographic/Getty Images, p. 4; Library of Congress, pp. 6–7 (LC-DIG-pga-02343); © Peter Harholdt/CORBIS, p. 8; © N. Currier/The Bridgeman Art Library/Getty Images, p. 9; Used with permission of Frank E. Sadowski Jr. of The Erie Canal web site, www.eriecanal.org, pp. 10, 15, 22–23, 25; © Albright-Knox Art Gallery/CORBIS, p. 11; © Art Resource, NY, p. 12; Detail of *The Erie Canal* by John William Hill, 1831, watercolor on paper, 16" x 20", courtesy of the Union College Permanent Collection, Union College, Schenectady, NY, p. 14; © SuperStock, Inc/SuperStock, p. 16; Robert N. Dennis Collection of Stereoscopic Views, Miriam and Ira D. Wallach Division of Art, Prints and Photographs, The New York Public Library, Astor, Lenox and Tilden Foundations, p. 17; The Art Archive/Culver Pictures, p. 18; Photography Collection, Miriam and Ira D. Wallach Division of Art, Prints and Photographs, The New York Public Library, Astor, Lenox and Tilden Foundations, p. 19; © North Wind Picture Archives, p. 24; © Philip Scalia/Alamy, p. 26; © Laura Westlund/Independent Picture Service, p. 28; © Andre Jenny/Alamy, p. 31.

Front Cover: © Andre Jenny/Alamy.